ABOUT THE AUTHOR

Rick Sanders, aka Willis the Poet, is an established comedy stand-up poet based in the mighty West Midlands. He is a regular headliner and featured poet on the flourishing spoken word scene across the UK, his sticky sausage-fingers in as many pies as he can.

You can find him running his mouth off at any event where there is a) an audience and b) a microphone. In between gigs he skulks in the dark recesses of abandoned buildings trying to think of funny things to write about, which is testament to the contents of this book really; a romp through the cerebral cortex of a man who writes humourous verse about pretty much anything and then inflicts it on unsuspecting poetry fans wherever he can.

The Top Secret Poetry
Notebook of
WILLIS THE POET

VERVE
POETRY PRESS
BIRMINGHAM

PUBLISHED BY VERVE POETRY PRESS
https://vervepoetrypress.com
mail@vervepoetrypress.com

FIRST PUBLISHED SEP 2021

Printed and bound in the UK
by ImprintDigital, Exeter

ISBN: 978-1-912565-46-7

Chapter illustrations by the author
Cartoons created by Andy Baker – andydoodlesbaker.com

This book is dedicated to all those people brave enough to stand up in front of a mic and share their work with the world - I salute you...

It is also dedicated to Jill, Zoe and Helen who are the most encouraging and understanding humans on this planet - without you, there would be nothing....

CONTENTS

FOOD

TRANSPORT

SPORT

LOVE

BEASTS

CAUTIONARY TALES AND NONSENSE

The ^top^ Secret Poetry Notebook of WILLIS THE POET

FOOD

BLACK MAGIC

It's 1983.
I'm at my Gran's watching ITV.
Gran's on the crochet
And what can I say -
It's dull.
Then there's a lull
In proceedings
As from the box
Opportunity Knocks
Goes to the ads.
After the one about sanitary pads,
A beautiful woman appears on screen,
A Duran Duran soundtrack adds to the scene,
As a bloke like James Bond appears out of nowhere,
All Gucci suit and swept-back hair.
He smooches over like a silver fox
Asking the question,
"Who knows the secret of the Black Magic box?"
My Gran looks up from her little knitted socks
And says, dead pan,
"Its's chocolates, you stupid man"

TEN A DAY

According to the government, 5 portions of fruit and veg a day is no longer enough and now only 10 portions will save us from dying 6 months earlier than if we had gone on a diet of pork belly smeared in goose fat.

Anyway, I thought I'd give it a go based on the government's recommended daily intake...

For breakfast
As well as a bowl of cereal
And two rounds of toast
I ate a whole cauliflower
Two portions, apparently

For lunch
As well as a healthy salad
Mixed leaves
Pulses
Grated carrot
I drank 14 litres of pureed spinach
Three portions, apparently

For tea
As well as corn on the cob
I ate potatoes, seven different ways
A bowl of sprouts
And a swede
Four portions, apparently
Finding myself one portion short
I ate eight bananas
That night
I shit the bed

PUDDING HAIKU

My Haiku about
Puddings contains spot on seven
Teen syllabubs

QUICHE LORRAINE

Quiche, Lorraine
It's somewhat niche, Lorraine
To have the egg-based pastry dish, Quiche Lorraine,
Named after yourself, Lorraine

TEABAG

Teabag, you're just too square
And even when you're round
You're just too cheap
80 for a pound
You're just common,
So unappealing,
Let's face it, you're just not organic, loose-leaf Darjeeling

A poem inspired by the very true story of a 74-Year-Old man arrested for giving his church congregation cookies laced with cannabis - my kind of church...

THE CANNABIS ANARCHIST

He pops up at social functions
Where there is a heartfelt need
For community based donations
And a lot of hungry mouths to feed

He brings his secret stash
Inside its Tupperware
His cookies baked with hash
For everyone to share

He's bought some lemon sherbet dabs
And stuck to all the dipping lollies
Hallucinogenic acid tabs
In about an hour they'll be off their trollies

Inside his chocolate éclair
His modified crème fraiche
Delivers a thousand yard stare
Brought on by crystal meth

He's put Uppers in the cuppas
Kibbles in the nibbles
Rohypnol in the Arctic Roll
And Wack in all the flap jack
There's Purple Haze in the canapes
Peruvian Flake in the carrot cake

He's even laced the margarine
With A grade street sourced Benzadrine
And to feed his need
For the sharing of joy
He's put Crazy Weed
In the savaloy

There's rock in all the rock cakes
Cake in all the other cakes
Temazepam in the breaded ham
Ketamine in the strawberry jam
He's spiked the tea with LSD
The sandwiches with Ecstacy
There's even Acapulco Red
In his freshly baked banana bread

He's a one man pharmacologist
The UKs Walter White
An all star Congregationalist
Doing what he thinks is right

So to help us all I've pulled some strings
And though is seems preposterous
He's down to do the catering
At the Tory Party Conference

TOBY CARVERY

Mary had a little lamb
A slice of roast beef
Turkey
Some boiled potatoes
Seasonal veg
Gravy
And a teaspoon of mint sauce

TUNNOCKS TEA CAKE

Who, in their right mind,
Doesn't love a Tunnocks Tea Cake.
I mean
For flips sake,
Fluffy marshmallow,
Biscuity base,
All enveloped in a chocolate case,
A tea-time treat
Wrapped up neat
In its shiny, silver foil
Perfect really
Unless you're allergic to sugar

YOU ARE WHAT YOU EAT
BREAKFAST

I am - scramblemashed budgerigar eggs on Korean artisanal sourdough toast slab, seasoned with the salt from elephant tears and hand crushed 1000 year old Aztec peppercorns

I am – cappucinilattemocharino, cold-brewed then refreshed through a coal-fired steamery, frothed with soyacurd enriched frozen Yak's milk essence, with dried Yasuka seaweed crushings

I am – piquant spiced sausagette, developed from hand-reared Etonian Old Black Spot piglings, air dried in vintage, French dovecotes

I am – organic-free, tofu infused, Bolivian beef tomatoes, press-ganged on to a bed of independent avocado salsa, with strawberry enriched despondency foam on the side

I am – condensed Alfalfa / Mango presse, squeezed between the hamstring and the calf of a trainee Sumo wrestler, served in an ironic reused Nutella glass tumbler

I am – hand-crafted grey pudding, enlivened with beaver fat, ingrediented using wild boar blood and crust shavings from individual, bespoke loaf sculptures, nestled in a reserve of Jurgenberry jus

I am – up-cycled muesli, sourced from "Cereal Killers of Dalston", importers of retro Swedish breakfast cereals from the 1970s, enhanced with tepid goat's milk and African Wild Bee honey extract, served in a WWII shellac bowl, eaten with a wooden spork whittled by a Princes Trust youth eco start-up not for profit

I am – hipster

TRANSPORT

LATE TRAIN

My train is late.
The announcement informs "disruptive passengers" and I start
a debate
With the chap next to me about how that can be
At twenty past 3 on a Wednesday afternoon.

We get our answer soon
As ten minutes later the train pulls in and
We can see them through the window
The hard-core, paramilitary wing
Of the Women's Institute.

They've come from their national conference
Fuelled on tea, jam and Victoria Sponge
The firebrand rhetoric of the collective
The Borg in twinset and pearls.
And it's clear that the cherry brandy,
In hip-flask discretion,
Has stoked quite a session.

They spill from the train and
A chorus of Jerusalem breaks out as
They jostle their way towards the exit.
I get struck on the knee by a flailing handbag
And I'm down, on the platform amidst a sea of A-line tweed
and sensible shoes.

As I struggle to my feet I hear their battle cry
"Come on ladies, let's re-take the city"
And I look up to see the ringleader, my Gran,
Sparking up the first Molotov Cocktail

BOY RACERS

I pulled up to the lights at The Lye Cross
Glancing across at the boy racer
Next to me
He stared back
Egged on by his mates
Engine revving
Drum n bass thumping
Testosterone pumping
I looked straight ahead
And thought to myself
Well, I'll race you if you like
But it's not going to be much of a contest
You in your Ford Ka
And me on my push bike

COMMUTER ONE

I see him every morning on his bike
Wheezing his way up the incline
And I'm inclined to wonder if he'd like
A car

When I don't have any commissions, I just like to make them up — it boosts my sense of self-worth. Here's one I made up for the Department of Transport, Road Safety. It's in 3 parts...

DEPARTMENT OF TRANSPORT ROAD SAFETY COMMISSION

Fox

I saw a fox last night
He ran across the road in front of me
Right there in front of me
Right in front of me
He was a Kamikaze fox
Do you know how I could tell?
Because he had a little Japanese flag
Wrapped around his forehead.
He was trying to make me swerve
Trying to force me off the road
It didn't work.
I just ran him down

Badger

I saw a badger last night
He ran across the road in front of me
Right there in front of me
Right in front of me
He was a Kamikaze badger
Do you know how I could tell?
Because he had a little Japanese flag
Wrapped around his forehead.
He was trying to make me swerve
Trying to force me off the road
It didn't work.
I just ran him down

Little Old Woman

I saw a little old woman last night
She ran across the road in front of me
Right there in front of me
Right in front of me
She was a Kamikaze little old woman
Do you know how I could tell?
Because she had a little Japanese flag
Wrapped around her forehead.
She was trying to make me swerve
Trying to force me off the road
It didn't work.
I braked just in time, because I was only doing 20
in a 30 mile an hour zone.

I think that commission's in the bag...

i JUST WANTED TO LET YOU KNOW

On the train to work last week,
I'm opposite a woman who keeps trying to
Sneak a peek
At my disarmingly good looks;
You couldn't write it in a book, I swear
The number of times that women of a certain age sit and stare.
It's embarrassing really,
But also quite appealing to know
That I've still got what it takes.
To turn heads,
While other blokes my age have retired to their sheds,
Out of harm's way,
Unable to play,
In the playing field,
On the swings and on the round-a-bouts.
But for me, no such doubts.
I'm all over the monkey bars,
Like, well, like a monkey,
Except in a suit.
Not a monkey suit of course,
I don't go to work in fancy dress!
But I digress.
She's still giving me the eye and
As we pull into Snow Hill, she's reached across and placed her hand
on my thigh,
"I hope you don't mind" she says
"But before you dash,
I just wanted to let you know,
You've got some food stuck in your tache!!"

ROOF RACK RAP

I bought a car with a roof rack
So I can go to IKEA for my flat pack
When half the bits are missing I can take it back
On the top of my Volvo, on my roof rack

I got my crew, chillin' in the back,
Emily, 5 and 3 year old Jack
and we're going down to Waitrose to get ourselves a stack
Of organic, Brazilian, free-range flapjack
Yeah the free-range flapjack

On the DAB we've got the Classic FM
Bangin' out the tunes, bringing on the mayhem
Mahler, Beethoven, Vivaldi's Four Seasons and
We're winding down the windows for no other reasons
Than to share with the world our musical taste
Invading your privacy, up in your face
And on the playlist amongst other things
Samuel Barber's Adagio for Strings
Samuel Barber's Adagio for Strings

At home the wife's on the Mumsnet
Looking for advice on where she can get
Vegitarian, Fairtrade, up-cycled yoghurt
Crafted by Mongolians living in a yurt
And the best place to source artisan fluff
For bringing up the hardwood floors to a high buff
Shine
And we've just got time
For a cheeky gin and tonic and an little glass of wine
Before our friends turn up, the ones who are arty
And we all sit down for a wicked dinner party
Yeah, a wicked dinner party

Carpaccio of beef and bilinis for starters
Rack of lamb main and banoffee pie for afters
I've eaten so much that I need a lie down
I get into my PJs and silk dressing gown
Retire to my snug, drop the Lazyboy back
And dream of all the things I can put on my roof rack
Yeah all the things I can put on my roof rack
All the ladies love a roof rack
I dream of all the things I can put on my roof rack

CAR PARK

I'm parking my car in the car park
The park for cars
But it's a little bit sad
There's no swings, no slides
Just round-a-bouts

SPORT

JOEY

My uncle Jimmy is a Bristol City fan
Match of the Day, chips and a can
Smoking like a train, swearing like a trooper
Every time the Robins are not so super duper

My auntie's in the kitchen nurse-maiding a gin
When out of the blue, my cousin Steph comes in
Declaring to us all that she's in the family way
And we better all get planning for her very special day

Now being of the left foot Catholic persuasion
A shotgun wedding as a difficult occasion
You have to save face and do the right thing
Knowing everybody knows that there's been a dirty fling

So they're all in attendance, the world and his missus
Half the WI helping out with the dishes
And it being part way through the current footie season
Uncle Jimmy cannot see any earthly reason
Why, on the dot of ten the telly isn't on
For Match of the Day and a theme tune sing-a-long

But what I haven't told you is that Jimmy has a pet
A budgerigar called Joey, the likes you've never met
He's an expert mimic, copying everything you say
And his favourite TV programme is Match of the Day

And as the music starts, he hops up on his perch
Checks his little mirror as if he's trying to search
For extra inspiration on how he wants to start
And then he wades on in, bless his little heart

"Pass the fucking ball, pass the fucking ball"
"What a load of crap, what a load of crap"
"You must be fucking blind, you must be fucking blind"
"Shit a brick, shit a brick"
"For fucks sake referee, for fucks sake referee"

Distracted by his bell, Joey stops to eat some Trill
The silence if deafening but soon begins to fill
With stifled coughs and shuffling feet
Followed by the bride's retreat
And Uncle Jimmy's beer filled joy
Shouting proudly, "that's my boy"

But Auntie Maud is spitting rage
And grabs poor Joey from his cage
Dislodging his cuttlefish, his little heart-shaped feeding dish
And swearing that she can't take any more
Evicts him out the window by the kitchen door

But do not fret at Joey's fate
He's often spotted at Ashton Gate
Down in the home supporters end
Where they seem to have adopted
Our little feathered friend
And when the final whistle blows
There's only one thing left to do
He's off to talk dirty, with his budgie mates at Bristol Zoo

FOOTBALLER FROM LYE

There was a footballer from Lye
Acursed with a wandering eye,
His wife caught him looking
And gave him a booking,
Red card and a nasty black eye!

PARKOUR

I watched them doing Parkour
I thought that it was pip
Now I'm down at A&E
With a broken hip

TABLE TENNIS

No matter what your mates might say on a Friday night
Down the pub after 10 pints of Snakebite
It's unlikely you'll be able
To play tennis
With a bedside table

OLYMPIC QUALIFICATION

I wrote to the International Olympic Committee
Only to be told
That I won't be competing for silver, bronze or gold
In my suggested sport of
Bedside table tennis

SNOOKER

Player 1
Chalky, chalk, chalk, chalk.
Break!
Clips the pack, clackity clack,
Off two cushions and a skulk
Past the blue
Back into baulk.

Player 2
Chalky, chalk, chalk, chalk.
Considering options,
Weighing up angles,
Wants to avoid a tactical tangle
With the loose reds.
Gets down on the shot and
Pot!
Nice screw back
Onto the black.

Chalky, chalk, chalk, chalk.
The black's pocketed,
Reds are rocketed in
One after the other
All with blacks
And the crowd are expecting the max
147.

Chalky, chalk, chalk, chalk.
Just the six colours to go and
He's nicely on to the yellow.
The green and brown are down,
The cue ball neatly through
For the blue.
But the pressure's really on
And a flighty mis-cue
Sends the blue
Slightly off line
To rattle in the jaws
(Nail-biting pause)
As it bounces from side to side
Then finally decides to drop.
Get in!!

Only the pink and black to go
But the crowd don't know
If he can hold his nerve
He's out of position on the pink,
Requiring the application of swerve.
But he sinks the pink with ease.
Quiet please!

Chalky, chalk, chalk, chalk.
You can hear a pin drop in the hall
As he lines up for the final ball.
His adrenalin pumping
He gives it a right thumping
A massive mistake
As the black careers into the jaws and
Takes off.

But the ball lands
Back on the table
With the force of the spin able
To bring the black to life.
It takes an UNBELIEVEABLE cannon
off the white,
Right into the middle pocket.

The crowd are on their feet,
Player 2 is on his knees,
Hugs and handshakes all round
The ref calls for "best of order please"
As he racks up the balls for the next
frame.
While he basks in maximum 147
heaven,
It's not the end of the game,
It's the best of eleven!

WICKET KEEPER

When I was thirteen
Or maybe fourteen
All I wanted to do was play cricket
More specifically to keep wicket
The wicket keeper
The keeper of the wickets
The man behind the sticks
Always in the thick of it
If there's a snick
Or a knick
He's all over it like an oil slick
Quicker than you can say quick
Lickety split
A flick of the ball
A lick of the lips
Then it's HOWZAT!
That's out

I loved the massive gloves
The little half-size pads
The fact there wasn't any running
While all the other lads
Were sprintity   sprint   sprint
In field   out field
Out field   in field
While the keeper
No risk of stitch
From his stroll up the pitch

in between overs
In his short sleeved pullover
All casual like
No need to get on his bike
They rarely ever got to bat
The proper batsmen did all that
Battity bat bat
While the keeper
He just sat back
Sun bathing on the balcony
With extra sarnies and a nice cup of tea
Yeah Wickie was the job for me
But it was not to be
My dreams were smashed
My hopes dashed
Stumped you might say
And it annoys me to this day
But to play for club and country
League test or twenty twenty
Twenty twenty vision was required
Otherwise you just weren't hired
And turning up for trials
In your milk bottle bottom NHS specs
Saw you straight to the bottom of the list
Early shower
slap on the wrist
For wasting the selectors time
After time
After time
But the test and county board came to it's senses
Now the jammy sods can all wear contact lenses

LOVE

BLIND DATE

I'm on a blind date looking for the one,
The special one,
Just like Jose Mourhino
Except a bit more smileo
And female.
I check my phone, no email,
Text or tweet,
No Instagram of her cold feet,
No missed call to say forget it all,
So I order another drink and keep an eye on the door.

On the radio they're playing Modern Love
And I'm not above
Recognising the irony.
Although I'm not a fan of David Bowie
Or is it Bowie,
Bowie, Bowie, Bowie, Bowie,
How am I supposed to knowie.
On the week he died I turned off Radio 6,
Sick to the back teeth of
Sycophantic platitudes
From across the hoards
I just got bored
Of being told
How he was bold,
Inspired a generation,
Warmed the cockles of a nation.
And if you don't like him, like me

Then you must be a knob, a Philistine, strange,
Or any combination of the three.
My date has arrived and I'm pleasantly surprised
She seems nice and has already apologised twice
For being late
And I think to myself "Wouldn't it be great
If this one didn't hurt".
But then she takes off her coat to reveal her David
Bowie T-Shirt

GIMPMASK

Gingerly dipping into the world of S&M
I purchased a G I M P M A S K
Mesmorised by the latex feel
Preoccupied by the rubbery smell
Mark my words though
An unattended mask is a kitten magnet
Snoozing in it's sweaty warmth
Keen to leave a fur-ball nestled in it's darkened folds

ROMEO AND JULIET

Verona party
Montagues and Capulets
He's in with a shout

They cannot marry
But they marry in secret
Now they are married

Before the nuptials
Romeo and Tybalt duel
Tybalt comes off worse

Under threat of death
Romeo leaves Verona
Paris makes his move

Friar Laurence plans
Juliet sets fake news death
They all fall for it

Romeo does too
Thinks she is dead tops himself
A bit premature

Juliet wakes up
Finds Romeo is dead now
So she tops herself

It's a tragedy
The moral of the story
At first double check

WE LOVE EACH OTHER

We love each other
Like mites love dust
Like a gambler loves to stick, not bust
Like a rocket loves thrust
Like a child loves to trust
The rope swing knot
As he approaches the zenith of the arc
Above the stinging nettle plot

We love each other
Like strawberries love cream
Like Martin Luther loves a dream
Like the Atlantic loves the gulf stream
Like a roof loves a beam
Like a freshly opened 240 page paper ream
Loves the journey through the internal workings
Of a photocopying machine

We love each other
Like a hoover loves to suck
Like pot loves luck
Like hoisin loves a nicely shredded duck
Like a dumper loves a dumper truck
Like a rusted up nut loves to be unstuck
By the liberal application of an oil based solution
Rather than being struck
By a hammer

We love each other
Like a bully loves school
Like Pythagoras loves the rule
That the square of the length of the hypotenuse
Is equal to the sum of the other two sides
Like a mechanic loves a tool
Like a kitchen counter loves a stool
Like a clown loves to play the fool
While secretly he's dying inside
From the need to constantly be happy
In the knowledge that
However many balloon sausage dogs he makes
He'll never have a real dog

We love each other
With the romantic call to arms that love conquers all
Is soon to be called out
Since you found out
That I slept with your sister

MY CARDIGAN

The thing I really like about my cardigan
Without a shadow of a doubt
Is that you can't accidentally put it on
Inside out
Unlike a jumper!

MORE ABOUT MY CARDIGAN

The thing I really like about my cardigan
Is that when it's warm I can
Open the buttons down the front of it
And generally waft it about a bit
You can't do that with a jumper!

EVEN MORE ABOUT MY CARDIGAN

The thing I really like about my cardigan
Is that after it's seen better days
You can re-use and recycle the buttons
In hundreds of different ways
There's no buttons on a jumper!

ODE TO THE PYLON

I love you pylon
You reach into the skylon
Magnificently highlon
You hardly have to trylon

You're eclectic
Geometric
Definitively electric
Your high-wire trapeze
A tempting towering tease
I want to climb you
Even though the health & safety rules define you
As life threatening
I'm betting
That the view
From you
Is awe inspiring

I love you pylon
As I spy you from afarlon
Through the window of my carlon
Stretched out across the landscape
Inviting escape
I'm urged to follow on
Until we reach the sub-station
Where we make the final connection
Sparks will flylon
You will be forever mylon
Pylon

BEASTS

CATS

I don't like cats, I have to confess
They come into my garden leaving their mess
On my lawn
They're the devils spawn
An acquired taste like marmite or sweetcorn.
They're malevolent, never benevolent
And their actions are rarely ever relevant
They sit around all day licking their bits
Their whole purpose in life seems solely to consist
Of wilful destruction
Malicious deconstruction
Like they're under the spell of demonic instruction
The wall paper hanging in the hall they like most
And the head of your bed
That they use as a scratching post
Cats, they've got the evil eye
Which they Satanically use every time that you try
To seek their affection
Or make a connection
Try and befriend them
Or reach out to send them
Your love, they bat back with vicious paws
Take the skin off your hand with razor sharp claws
They've got fleas, they carry disease,
They'll give you rabies, asthma and all the other allergies
And when they're not bringing half dead birds into you house
They'll leave a partly eaten squirrel or a dead-headed mouse
In your shoe, or on the floor of the loo

Which you'll slip on when you go for a midnight poo
If I had my way I'd put em all in a sack
A couple of bricks then it's onto my back
Off down the cut where it's sink or swim
But they're well weighed down so I think
That it's sink.
I hate cats, but what I didn't realise
Is that they're organised
They've got their own protection league
The Cats Protections League
They're untouchable, pretty irreproachable
I really wouldn't class them as approachable
If you bring a stick, they'll bring a knife
If you bring a gun, they'll kidnap your wife
Sending bits of her ear back in an envelope
Advising that respect is your only hope
The message is clear, know your place
In the pecking order of the cat master race.
So it's fair to say
That on any given day
I don't like cats.
I'm more of a dog man.

THE FOUR HORSEMEN OF THE APOCALYPSE

gallopy, gallopy, gallopy, gallopy,
gallopy, gallopy, gallop,
they sprint like dogs
to reach the bogs
dicky tummies from dodgy scallops

SAUSAGE DOG HAIKU

My Dad's sausage dog
Resembled a fire side log
Now, it's a hot dog

LOST CAT

A colleague at work told me she had lost her cat
And it was only after I had asked
"Have you looked behind the sofa?"
That she said,
"No lost, as in dead"

GOLDiLOCKS

Oh Goldilocks this just won't do
Breakering and entering
Pilfering and porridging
Feckless freelance foraging

Too hotty, too coldilocks
Too biggy, too tinylocks
Too softy, too harsh
You spoilt little mardy arse
Grumbling selfishly, apparently helplessly
Through the bear-free house of orphan opportunity

But while you slumber Goldilocks
In baby bear's pink beddie socks
The alpha male has got your scent
Hell bent on having his revenge
To avenge the porridgy puddle, the shattered stool
That took him weeks to make at bear night school
And up the stairies he's a creeping
To slay you while you lie a sleeping

But bear has underestimated your resolve
Your in-built knack to problem solve
And the fact that being somewhat handilocks
You are armed at once with your pistols cocked, locked and
loaded, the shots explode extinguishing the Ursa Major thus
With just the minimum of fuss

The grizzly's gizzards glisten on the floor
As you listen for more approaching paws
But mother bear and babylocks have seized their chance
With daddy gone they're off to live in France
To open up an AIRBEARBNB
Where they can both live happily ever after

DOG ASSISTED THERAPY

Pat the dog
Pat the dog
That's dog assisted therapy

Stroke the dog
Stroke the dog
That's dog assisted therapy

Scratch the dog behind the ear
That's dog assisted therapy

Cuddle the dog
Cuddle the dog
That's dog assisted therapy

Love the dog
Love the dog
That's dog assisted therapy

Take the dog for a nice long walk
That's dog assisted therapy

Groom the dog
Groom the dog
That's dog assisted therapy

Shake his paw
Shake his paw
That's dog assisted therapy

Roll him over and tickle his tummy
That's dog assisted therapy

Kiss the dog
Kiss the dog
That's dog assisted therapy

Fetch the ball
Fetch the ball
That's dog assisted therapy

But picking up shit in a plastic bag
Where's the fucking therapy in that??

CAUTIONARY TALES AND NONSENSE

LiTTER PiCKER

He is a litter picker
Picking litter
With his litter-picking sticker
His little pointy stick for sticking through the litter.
He has a black bin liner for putting litter in
Coz the lazy litter louts can't be assed to use the bin.
But he's not bitter
He just gets better
As a litter picker upper
To earn his bread and butter.
He sees it as art
Cathartically piling
Methodically filing
The day's daily droppings
While secretly compiling
An assassins creed
For the unsuspecting in-breeds
That do their dirty deeds.
His list is extensive
His weapons inexpensive
As he whiles away the days
Concocting different ways
To maim and shame the litterati.
For a straight paper drop he'll stick you with his stick
In between the ribs, it'll be nice and quick
For confectionary wrapping, it's a double knee-capping
For a cigarette butt, it's a knife to the gut

If you leave plastic, well things get drastic
He'll whip out your eyes with a piece of strong elastic
And for the cardinal sin of not binning your gum
He'll start with the thumb screws
Torture and abuse
With his double LP of the singer Julie Andrews
And then it's on with the concrete shoes
And a one-way ticket to the underwater blues.
It won't happen of course
It just keeps him amused
While he's picking up litter
In a town near you.

HENRY Viii

On 11th June 1509
Henry VIII married Catherine of Aragon
The paragon
Of Spanish virtue
The schoolday rhyme
Divorced
Beheaded
Died
Divorced
Beheaded
Survived
Could have been so much more succinct
If they'd have just got on

READING FESTIVAL

Am I the only one to think
That words can be misleading?
I'm here a Reading Festival
Wondering where all the books are?

FAT BALLS

There's nothing I enjoy more than hanging out my fat balls
Delicious dangling dumplings my fat balls
Tempting tasty titbits my fat balls
Attracting all the birds from far and wide my fat balls
But yesterday a squirrel got on my fat balls
He chewed through the stringy sack of my fat balls
And now my fat balls
Are flat balls

SWINGS

When I was seven
I was pretty sure that I could fly.
So I thought I'd give it a try,
Off the swings in the park behind my house.
Turns out, I couldn't.

SPANISH INQUISITION

Nobody expects the Spanish Inquisition
Except, perhaps, the Spanish

RICHARD iii

I went to polytechnic in Leicester
And it turns out that for one whole semester
I was walking over Richard the 3rd,
On my way, ironically you might say,
To my lectures on "the limitations of the
English Monarcy in the later middle ages"

THE ALPHABET

A is for Alphabet
There you go, sorted

PASSION KILLER

If you're going to impress on your big night out
When you're in with a chance, when you're in
with a shout
From experience, just do a quick double check
That you haven't put your pants on
Inside out

MY GRANDAD

My niece and her boyfriend
Decided that for their marriage
They'd go all out on a horse-drawn carriage
My Grandad said "They've more money than sense"
The grumpy bastard.

For Divali my neighbours two doors down
Lit up the sky, they really went to town
On seeing the sight
My Grandad said "It's not bloody bonfires night.
The grumpy bastard.

For my 40th birthday we went for a meal
A nice gastro pub, the real deal
And it being trendy and full of style
Your food was served on a big slate tile.
My Grandad said "What's wrong with a plate, for fucks sake?"
The grumpy bastard

The very next day after the Summer solstice
My Grandad would always say
"The nights are drawing in"
The grumpy bastard

This poem is about the perils of lunchtime drinking and might be based on a true story...

BIG MAC FRIES TO GO

I'm standing in the queue thinking what do I want
I want Big Mac, fries to go
I'm next in line so I say to the bloke
I want Big Mac, fries to go
He looks at me blank so I say real slow
I want a Big Mac and fries to go
Still no reaction, he's dead behind the eyes
So I repeat myself
I want a Big Mac and fries

Without explanation
He vacates his station
Returns with a chap in a shirt and tie
And I wonder if this fella
In managerial guise
Will be able to give me
My Big Mac and fries

"I'm sorry" he says, "we don't have Mac and fries"
Which I'm telling you now came as quite a surprise
And I'm about to get lairy and have a good shout
When he holds up his hand and politely points out
I'm in Poundland

ACKNOWLEDGEMENTS

My thanks go out to all those people that bring poetry to the world; the writers, the performers, the programmers, the printers, the publishers, the promoters, the YouTubers, the Instagramers, the creators, the readers, the venue managers, the audiences, the coffee shop owners, the publicans, the festival directors, the writing groups, the reading groups, the booksellers, the illustrators, the event managers, the fringe organisers, the listeners, the DJs, the film-makers, the producers, the volunteers, the pod-casters, the sound engineers, the friends and the families, the notebook makers and the person who invented the pencil. You all have a part to play and without you the world would be a soul-less piece of rock.

My extra-special thanks go to Stuart at Verve Poetry Press for having some sort of drug-induced vision in wanting to publish this book. He has staked his substantial reputation on publishing the random and often inexplicable musings of a comic poet and for that I will forever hold a little piece of him in my heart.

Thank you Jill, Zoe and Helen for all your support, your intelligence and your love. You have stood by and watched a barely competent man's descent into idiocy in front of complete strangers without even a hint of regret or the merest suggestion of a full refund and for that, you should be rightly applauded.

And lastly...
My thanks to all the poetry promoters, who will now take this book as recognition of the brilliance of Willis the Poet and book him on a regular, repeating basis, making him the wealthiest living poet working the circuit today, until senility takes it's ultimate grip on the mind of this wayward, yet lovable "poet-next-door" journeyman.

ABOUT VERVE POETRY PRESS

Verve Poetry Press is a quite new and already award-winning press that focused initially on meeting a local need in Birmingham - a need for the vibrant poetry scene here in Brum to find a way to present itself to the poetry world via publication. Co-founded by Stuart Bartholomew and Amerah Saleh, it now publishes poets from all corners of the UK - poets that speak to the city's varied and energetic qualities and will contribute to its many poetic stories.

Added to this is a colourful pamphlet series, many featuring poets who have performed at our sister festival - and a poetry show series which captures the magic of longer poetry performance pieces by festival alumni such as Polarbear, Matt Abbott and Genevieve Carver.

The press has been voted Most Innovative Publisher at the Saboteur Awards, and has won the Publisher's Award for Poetry Pamphlets at the Michael Marks Awards.

Like the festival, we strive to think about poetry in inclusive ways and embrace the multiplicity of approaches towards this glorious art.

www.vervepoetrypress.com
@VervePoetryPres
mail@vervepoetrypress.com